INSTRUCTOR'S MANUAL

BUSINESSWATCH

ANSWER KEY

Keith Maurice

Intermediate
ESL Video
Library

Susan Stempleski
Series Editor

PRENTICE HALL REGENTS
Englewood Cliffs, New Jersey 07632

Acquisitions Editor: **Nancy Leonhardt**
Manager of Development Services: **Louisa Hellegers**
Development Editor: **Barbara Barysh**
Editorial Production / Design Manager: **Dominick Mosco**
Production/Composition: **Jan Sivertsen**
Production Coordinator: **Ray Keating**
Cover Supervisor: **Merle Krumper**
Interior Design: **Function Thru Form**
Technical Support: **Molly Pike Riccardi**

©1994 by PRENTICE HALL REGENTS
Prentice–Hall, Inc.
A Paramount Communications Company
Englewood Cliffs, New Jersey 07632

Video material © 1994 American Broadcasting
Companies, Inc. All rights reserved.

ABC Distribution Company

Printed in the United States of America
10   9   8   7   6   5   4   3   2   1

ISBN 0-13-503970-3

Prentice-Hall International (UK) Limited, *London*
Prentice-Hall of Australia Pty. Limited, *Sydney*
Prentice-Hall Canada Inc., *Toronto*
Prentice-Hall Hispanoamericana, S.A., *Mexico*
Prentice-Hall of India Private Limited, *New Delhi*
Prentice-Hall of Japan, Inc., *Tokyo*
Simon & Schuster Asia Pte, Ltd., *Singapore*
Editora Prentice-Hall do Brasil, Ltda., *Rio de Janeiro*

SEGMENT 1

WAL-MART VS. BRATTLEBORO, VT

BEFORE YOU WATCH

PREDICTING
Possible answers:

SIGHTS	WORDS
1. Wal-Mart	change
2. Brattleboro, Vermont	chain stores
3. shoppers	pricing
4. small business	competition
5. small business owners	discounts

KEY WORDS
Sample sentences:
1. IBM is a *Goliath* in the computer industry.
2. In times of recession, many *retailing* businesses must struggle to survive.
3. The 1980's and 90's have been a time of great *expansion* for many companies in southeast Asia.
4. One of the big political issues in the U.S. in the 90's centers around the matter of *tax revenues*. Should the government increase tax revenues or cut spending to deal with the deficit?
5. The mom-and-pop variety store in Brattleboro will suffer much *leakage* because of Wal-Mart's expansion into the area.
6. The rise and expansion of chain stores has had much *impact* all over the world.
7. The *super discount stores* have had a large, negative impact on smaller, family-owned stores in many countries.
8. Apple Computer might be an *exception* to the rule that a small company cannot compete against the Goliaths by using a different type of technology.

GETTING THE MAIN IDEA

What?	*Building new stores*
Where?	*In small cities and towns ignored by other major chain stores*
Why?	*It could harm their businesses*
How?	*By giving customers more and better service; by adjusting store hours; by making credit available to local residents*

WHAT'S MISSING

1. retailing
2. empire
3. recession
4. earnings

5. focus
6. store
7. merchants
8. Davids

WHAT DO YOU SEE?

1. pick-up truck
2. construction workers
3. river
4. tree-covered mountain
5. small town
6. small bridge
7. casually dressed shoppers

TRUE OR FALSE?

1. F Wal-Mart is expanding into the state of *New Hampshire*.
2. T
3. F Brattleboro is an *old* town.
4. F According to the Iowa study, *60* percent of Wal-Mart's sales comes at the expense of local businesses.
5. T

LISTENING FOR DETAILS

1. c	5. c
2. b	6. a & b
3. a	7. c
4. b	8. a

AFTER YOU WATCH

LANGUAGE POINT

1. b
2. a
3. d
4. c
5. f
6. e

VOCABULARY CHECK

1. expenses	5. writer
2. benefit from	6. put money on
3. convenience	7. switch
4. adjust	8. pleased

READING

1. To get the best possible retailing mix for the target market
2. Juggle the retailing mix to keep it in balance with the target market
3. a. Product: Items carried (product or service)—brands, sizes, etc.
   b. Place: Location/where exactly should it be— town/country, alone/mall, etc.
   c. Promotion: Advertising, selling, sales, etc.
   d. Price: Pricing alternating
   e. Personality: The way the store is perceived by the customer
4. Essential to project an appropriate personality.

SEGMENT 2

NEW TRENDS IN RETAILING

BEFORE YOU WATCH

PREDICTING
Answers will vary.

KEY WORDS
1. e
2. g
3. f
4. b
5. c
6. a
7. d

WHILE YOU WATCH

GETTING THE MAIN IDEA

How?	*Stores are offering discounts; shoppers are spending less*
Who/winners?	*Giant discount stores, wholesale clubs, catalog sales, television shopping, and shopping by computer*
Who/losers?	*Retail (department) stores, fancy stores*

CHECKING WHAT YOU HEAR

	BEFORE	NOW
1.	√	
2.	√	
3.		√
4.		√
5.	√	
6.		√
7.	√	
8.		√
9.		√
10.		√

NOTETAKING

1. 8-10 %
2. 30 %
3. Catalog sales, television shopping, and shopping by computers
4. Discount stores
5. Consumers are spending less and trading down

INFORMATION MATCH

1. c
2. d
3. b
4. c
5. d
6. a

AFTER YOU WATCH

LANGUAGE POINT

1. Before, consumers looked toward the top of the line.
   Now, they focus on the bottom line.

2. Before, department stores were popular.
   Now, giant discount stores are more popular.

3. Before, people were much less conservative.
   Now, they watch what they spend.

4. Before, people were watching for fads.
   Now, they are watching for investment clothing.

5. Before, people were inclined to buy on impulse.
   Now, they are less inclined to do so.

6. Before, it was common to have someone meet you at the front door and make sure you got treated properly, make sure the clothes fit you properly.
   Now, those days are disappearing.

VOCABULARY CHECK

Shopping Criteria	Store Appearance	Sale and Profit Terms	Types of Shopping
style	glitzy	volume	retail
color	fancy	turnover	catalog
price	no-frills	margin	wholesale
service			outlet

WORD FORMS (in text)

NOUN DESCRIBING PERSON	VERB	NOUN DESCRIBING ACTION
shopper	shop	**shopping**
consumer	**consume**	**consumption**
retailer	**retail**	retail, retailing
discounter	**discount**	**discount, discounting**
trader	trade	**trade, trading**
investor	**invest**	investment
salesperson, seller	**sell**	sales

READING

1. d
2. f
3. g
4. b
5. a
6. h
7. e
8. i
9. c

SEGMENT 3
TOO MANY TIRES

BEFORE YOU WATCH

PREDICTING

1. Why are there too many tires?
2. How many tires are there?
3. Where are the tires?
4. What can we do with them?
5. How do we get rid of them?

KEY WORDS

Sample sentences:
1. There was a funny *commercial* on TV last night about tires.
2. A large company needs to communicate well with its *dealerships*.
3. Gas station owners often take old tires out back and *dump* them.
4. *Entrepreneurs* are now offering new solutions to these old problems.
5. They're going to dump the old tires into a huge *incinerator* and burn them.
6. Here is *private enterprise* at its best, turning a problem into a solution and making a profit doing it.
7. It's the *"not in my backyard"* problem. The neighbors say, "Great idea, but not here."
8. The factory uses much *pollution* control equipment to help keep the environment clean.

WHILE YOU WATCH

GETTING THE MAIN IDEA

Who?	*American car owners*
What?	*Discarding their old tires*
Where?	*At gas stations*
Why/problems?	*The gas stations have nowhere to dump the tires; tires take hundreds of years to decompose; tires can easily catch fire; piles of tires are ugly*
What/solution?	*Burning the tires to make electrical energy*
Why/ not used?	*People don't want the factories near where they live*

WHAT'S MISSING

1. million
2. tires
3. fraction
4. thrown
5. billion
6. 200
7. earth
8. someone

WHAT DO YOU SEE?

1 A pick-up truck moving in the desert.
3 A mechanic taking a tire off a vehicle.
5 The reporter talking to a truckstop worker.
6 Large "flocks" of birds flying over a garbage dump.
2 A pick-up truck moving in the snow.
7 Garbage being moved at a garbage dump.
4 A couple of tires being dumped in back of a gas station.

NOTETAKING

1. Put them in the back
2. Dumps no longer accept tires, landfills don't have much room, and tires don't decompose
3. Catching fire
4. Shred them and sell the pieces as fuel; cut them up and use the pieces to make fishing nets; grind them into a powder that is used to make carpet backing and hockey pucks
5. 10 cents
6. 150 tires deep
7. Rattlesnakes live in some of the tires
8. Dump the tires into a huge incinerator and burn them to make electricity
9. 15,000
10. Heat it

TRUE OR FALSE

1. F Each tire is equal to *2 ½* gallons of oil.
2. T
3. F Many cities and communities all over the country *don't* want these kinds of energy factories.
4. F The factory *does not* produce a bad smell.
5. T
6. F The equipment has been used in Germany for *14* years.
7. T
8. F A similiar plant is *not* being built in New Hampshire because the local people *don't* want it.

AFTER YOU WATCH

LANGUAGE POINT

1. *are discarded*
2. is thrown
3. is exposed
4. are buried
5. are used
6. are converted
7. is used
8. are adopted

VOCABULARY CHECK

1. b
2. b
3. a
4. a
5. b
6. c
7. b
8. a

READING

1. Main idea (The first sentence in the first paragraph):

   . . . The problems of the business community have often seemed to be very different from the problems of the environment.

2. Examples of industries with environmental problems:

INDUSTRY	PROBLEMS
a. Lumber	deforestation
b. Auto	tire dumps, air pollution
c. Oil and chemical	leaks, accidents, storage, pollution
d. Computer	water pollution

3. Implications that can occur:
   a. Business: environmental impact on economic prosperity
   b. Workers: job loss
   c. Consumers: acceptance of environmentally sound products
      acceptance of higher prices for environmentally sound products
   d. National governments: impact of different environmental standards on trade issues

4. Examples of solutions:
   a. Power: solar and wind
   b. Transportation: electric cars
   c. Widespread trend: recycling
   d. McDonald's: reducing its use of thick containers
   e. Thomas Ceramic: Transforming garbage into bricks for construction.

SEGMENT 4
DISNEY'S LONG-TERM STRATEGIES

BEFORE YOU WATCH

PREDICTING
Answers will vary.

KEY WORDS
Sample sentences:
1. Disney's *revenues* from Disney World, Florida are an important part of the company's overall profit picture.
2. The *financing* for many large projects is difficult to arrange.
3. Disney's *equity* in any venture is an important part of the business arrangement.
4. In bad economic times, many small companies have major *cash flow* problems.
5. The *shareholders* in some large multinational companies, e.g., General Motors, have not been very happy the last few years.
6. Disney expects a solid *net income* from Euro Disney.
7. An issue many nations and communities have to face is how many *incentives* should be offered to outside companies to establish business operations in those locations.
8. Governments sometimes give *tax breaks* to outside companies that build factories in the area.

WHILE YOU WATCH

GETTING THE MAIN IDEA

Who?	*The Walt Disney Company*
What?	*An entertainment complex called Euro Disney*
Where?	*20 miles east of Paris*
How much?	*$4 billion*
What/unusual?	*The Walt Disney Company invested only $140 million in the project but will own 49% of the equity.*

IDENTIFYING WHAT YOU SEE (Matching time to image seen)

1. d
2. a
3. e
4. b

5. g
6. f
7. c

LISTENING FOR DETAILS

1. b
2. b
3. a

4. c
5. a
6. c

NOTETAKING

1.
Disney's investment	$140,000,000
Total investment	$4,000,000,000
Disney's equity	49%
Disney's management fee	3%
Disney's royalties	7.5%
Disney's cash flow	As much as 50%

2. Incentives of the French government to Disney
   a. Extending a commuter line
   b. Loan guarantees
   c. Tax breaks
   d. Special stop for France's high-speed train

MAKING TRUE SENTENCES

1. One of the job seekers believes *that it is unfair for Disney to ask you to take your nose ring out.*
2. Some people believe *that Disney will bring "hamburger culture to the land of haute culture".*
3. The labor representative believes *that the French government won the contract at the expense of many laws and social rights.*
4. Mr. Fitzpatrick, the Disney executive, does not believe *that France is an old lady terrified of a mouse.*

CHECKING WHAT YOU HEAR

1. √
2. —
3. √
4. —

5. √
6. —
7. √

LANGUAGE POINT
1. *It's important to remember that* Disney has a worldwide reputation for excellent management.
2. *Please remember that* the government is taking a relatively small risk for the opportunity to get large benefits.
3. *You must realize that* it's taken many, many years to gain these rights and now they are just being thrown away.
4. *I think it's important to note that* Disney image is a key part of its success and it must be protected and upheld.

VOCABULARY CHECK

Owner Terms	Revenue Terms	Government Actions	Marketing Terms	Bargaining Terms
equity	net income	tax break	publicity	threat
stock	royalties	incentives	TV coverage	bidding war
investment	management fee	loan guarantees	blitz	drive a hard bargain

READING
1.

COSTS	BENEFITS
European companies losing competitiveness	jobs
overcapacity	advanced manufacturing techniques
workforce cuts	more productivity
industrial unrest	reduce trade imbalance with Japan

2. The opponents feel that their factories are just Japanese "screwdriver" plants assembling components made in Japan.
3. Japanese manufacturers respond to this criticism by 'increasing' local content.
4. To enhance local content while attaining world competitiveness.

SEGMENT 5

THE INTERNATIONAL AIRLINE INDUSTRY

BEFORE YOU WATCH

PREDICTING

Sample questions:
1. How is the industry changing?
2. Which airlines are doing well?
3. Which airlines are doing poorly?
4. What was the industry like before?
5. What will the industry be like in the future?

KEY WORDS

1. e
2. g
3. f
4. h
5. a
6. c
7. b
8. d

CATEGORIZING TERMS

TERMS OF WORKING TOGETHER	TERMS RELATED TO GOVERNMENT	TERMS ABOUT PROBLEMS
pooling	reform	noncompetitive
join hands	state-owned	demise
consolidation	national flag carrier	failure

WHILE YOU WATCH

GETTING THE MAIN IDEA

Who?	Airline companies
What?	Moving toward international mergers and industry consolidation
Where?	Europe
Why?	In order to expand their systems globally and to be able to compete with the stronger American airline companies

WHAT'S MISSING?

1. travelling
2. reason
3. recover
4. failure
5. bankruptcy
6. overseas

NOTETAKING

1. a. On time
   b. Service
   c. Reliability
   d. Great chocolate
2. There is a tremendous fight on the North Atlantic; it will last another year or two.
3. American, Delta, and United.
4. a. The emergence of stronger American carriers
   b. Europe 1992 reforms and deregulation
5. A wave of mergers

INFORMATION MATCH

1. b	5. c
2. a	6. d
3. a, b, & c	7. d
4. a	

TRUE OR FALSE

1. T
2. F Donald Carty things there will have to be *a disassociation* if the marketplace is going to survive internationally.
3. T
4. F Richard Leone thinks JFK *will* survive this fallout.
5. T
6. T
7. F The partnership involving Delta Airlines, Swissair and Singapore Airlines *saved* money.
8. T

AFTER YOU WATCH

LANGUAGE POINT
Answers will vary.

VOCABULARY CHECK
1. expansion
2. possibility
3. finish
4. cooperation
5. reform
6. fail
7. join with
8. inequitable

READING
1. (any two of these four): loyal, picky, desperate, happy
2. service
3. North American (none)
   European (none)
   Asia-Pacific (double)
4. Big shortage of flight openings
5. Japanese: Give Japanese carriers more slots
   U.S.: Move to protect U.S. airlines
6. a. Japanese: Airlines are emblems of national power
   b. American: Air travel revenues are important to U.S. economy
7. a. cultural seminars
   b. roomier seats +
   c. "Connoisseur class" (employers to study Japanese culture)
   d. compact disk players
   e. Japanese food
   f. orchids
      (extra) a marketing blitz
8. a. U.S. airline inroads
   b. pilot shortage
   c. union threats to strike
   d. spending race
   e. Asian carriers with weaker unions and lower overhead

SEGMENT 6

NORTH AMERICAN FREE-TRADE AGREEMENT

PREDICTING
Sample items:
1. Conditions of the agreement
2. Advantages of the agreement
3. Disadvantages of the agreement
4. Views from business leaders
5. Views from workers
6. Countries involved

KEY WORDS
Sample definitions:
1. *negotiators:* people who bargain with each other, for example buyers and sellers, trying to get the best possible agreement for their side

2. *prospect:* the potential or possibility of something happening

3. *trade barriers:* devices a government uses to control against too many foreign products coming into the country

4. *proponents:* people who believe that an action will be beneficial

5. *lax standards:* very loose and weak guidelines or rules

6. *trade surplus:* when a country sells more abroad than it buys from abroad.

7. *domestic content:* the amount of a product that is made in country and not imported from abroad.

8. *tariffs:* taxes against foreign-made products

WHILE YOU WATCH

GETTING THE MAIN IDEA

Who?	*(Negotiators for) Mexico, Canada, and the U. S.*
What?	*Agree on the terms of the North American Free Trade Agreement (NAFTA)*
Where?	*Washington, D.C.*
Why/against?	*They think American jobs and industries will be lost; they question Mexico's commitment to the environment; they think it will result in bigger trade deficits.*
Why/for?	*They think it will create new job opportunities, increase exports, boost the U.S. economy, and open up new markets in Latin American countries.*
What problems?	*Mexico will become export oriented to U.S.; U.S. will acquire larger trade deficit, loss of American jobs*

CHECKING WHAT YOU HEAR

How much do these workers earn?	$65 a week	$8 an hour	$0.86 an hour	$1300 a week
Auto workers for Ford in Mexico City	√			
Auto workers in Detroit				√
Solderers for General Dynamics in Mexico			√	
Solderers in the U.S.		√		

TRUE OR FALSE?

1. F It's *no surprise* that the prospect of a North American Free Trade Agreement has many in the U.S. worried.
2. F Only fools *wouldn't* move manufacturing plants to pay 10 cents in labor for every dollar they are spending now.
3. T
4. F Frankly Jacobs, CEO of Falcon Products, says that the Mexican workers are *unsophisticated* and the educational system is *not* fabulous.
5. T

LISTENING FOR DETAILS

1. c   5. c
2. c   6. a
3. a   7. b
4. b

NOTETAKING

JEFF FAUX	STEPHEN AUG	JOHN CREGAN
1. training	1. environmental standards	1. trade deficits
2. health care	2. rules of origin provisions	2. job loss
		3. rules of origin and domestic content requirements

AFTER YOU WATCH

LANGUAGE POINT
Answers will vary.

VOCABULARY CHECK

1. destroy   5. promoted
2. opportunity   6. excuse
3. taxes   7. support
4. put aside   8. reward

READING

1. It is a symbol of openness and market liberalization to Europeans. To people outside Europe, it appears as a closed market.

2. a. To break down barriers in commerce
   b. To revitalize European industry to compete with Japan and the U.S.
3. internal freedom coupled with external protection.
4. a. anti-dumping action—-flexible protectionism
   b. reciprocal deals—-special deals with other regions
   c. quotas—-limits to how many imports are accepted
5. The author is against protectionist devices.

SEGMENT 7
CORPORATE QUALITY IN THE U.S.

BEFORE YOU WATCH

PREDICTING
Answers will vary.

KEY WORDS
1. e	5. a
2. c	6. f
3. g	7. b
4. h	8. d

WHILE YOU WATCH

GETTING THE MAIN IDEA

What?	*They lost business to the Japanese.*
Why?	*Their products got lower quality ratings than Japanese products.*
How/Corning Glass?	*By putting in a total quality system*
How/Eastman Kodak?	*By using teamwork and expanding worker responsibility*
What/problems?	*Meeting production quotas, cost for warranty, lack of understanding on Wall Street*

WHAT'S MISSING?

1. deficits
2. foreign
3. buying
4. television
5. step

IDENTIFYING WHAT YOU SEE

1. f
2. b
3. a
4. c
5. d
6. e

CHECKING WHAT YOU HEAR

1. —
2. √
3. √
4. —
5. √
6. —

NOTETAKING

1. The automobile
2. Expectations for the quality of some cars, e.g., Cadillac and Mercedes, were higher than for other cars.
3. The quality had improved so much they were as good as those made elsewhere.
4. They had developed a lot of problem areas and there was still a significant gap between American quality and some of the leading Japanese imports.

INFORMATION MATCH

1. b
2. d
3. c

4. b
5. a
6. c
7. d
8. a

LISTENING FOR DETAILS

1. c
2. a
3. b
4. a
5. c

AFTER YOU WATCH

LANGUAGE POINT

1. (answer given in lesson)
2. If you *didn't turn out* shoddy products, the customers *wouldn't* disappear.
3. If you *think* only about the domestic market, your competitors *will* go right by you.
4. If we *maintained* a total quality management system, we *would become* the best in the world.
5. If the company *makes* the improvements, it *will still be* in business.

VOCABULARY CHECK

1. a
2. b
3. b
4. c
5. a
6. a
7. b
8. c

READING

1. Giving customers what they want, when they want it, consistently
2. The theories are not easily applied.
3. G.M. invested heavily into automating its production line
4. No
5. Quality circles
6. Most failed.
7. Most lacked management support.
8. It set up ways to measure customer service.
9. Yes
10. It became buried in paperwork.
11. It scrapped many of the changes.
12. Employee participation, leadership, and measurement
13. a. Departments should see each other as customers.
    b. Managers should act more like coaches.
    c. Companies should train employees in problem-solving.

SEGMENT 8

CHRYSLER/FORD PROFITS

BEFORE YOU WATCH

PREDICTING

SIGHTS	WORDS
Chrysler and Ford executives	profit margins
Chrysler and Ford vehicles	market
automobile production plants	prices
automobile sales people	production
automobile showrooms	cars

KEY WORDS

1. red ink: financial losses
2. profit margins: percentage of profits of sales
3. disparities: gaps or differences

4. comparably equipped: containing equipment of similar quality and features
5. market share: the percentage of the total market sales that one company has
6. consumer confidence: the positive feelings that consumers have about the economy that lead them to buy.
7. modest: rather low, not very high
8. recession: bad economic times, e.g., when a nation's industries are doing well

WHILE YOU WATCH

GETTING THE MAIN IDEA

Who?	Ford and Chrysler Motor Companies
What?	Showing profits and competing for the marketplace
Why?	Jeeps, lightweight trucks, and minivans are impressing car buyers
How?	They've had to raise prices to maintain profits and this has created a price disadvantage

WHAT'S MISSING?
1. red
2. black
3. profit
4. 178
5. economy

WHO'S WHO

Who . . .?	Michael Towers	Farrell Furst	Jeff Monninger
1. thinks the new Jeep has a unique design	√		
2. thinks the Jeep rides great & is comfortable		√	
3. likes the fact that the Jeep is American	√		
4. is very pleased with large volume of sales			√
5. is surprised by how popular the Jeep is			√
6. thinks the Jeep has everything you want		√	

MAKING TRUE SENTENCES
1. Stephen Aug reports that Chrysler's line of lightweight trucks has been a strong profit center.
2. Joseph Phillippi notes that there are wide disparities in price between Japanese and U.S. vehicles.
3. Mary Ann Keller states that Chrysler earns about $5,000 in profit per minivan.
4. Albert Vitarelli says that it's the Big Three again and they're coming out with good stuff.
5. Stephen Aug reports that a comparably equipped Saturn is $3,000 less than a Honda Accord.
6. Stephen Aug reports that profit margins on truck sales are almost double those on car sales.

NOTETAKING
1. Down
2. Need to replace used vehicles (cars are beginning to wear out)
3. Little benefit

28

4. Negatively (Feels Ford is growing at a low rate and there aren't future signs to help this situation.)
5. He can hardly believe that it is growing at such a low rate.

AFTER YOU WATCH

LANGUAGE POINT
Sample sentences:
1. *Unlike* the improved situation at Ford, General Motors continues to struggle.
2. *In contrast to* car sales following previous recessions, car sales in 1992 have been sluggish.
3. *Unlike* Chrysler's solid profit margin in the second quarter, it had reported losses in previous quarters.
4. *In contrast to* the large profit margins on truck sales, profit margins on car sales are only half as much.
5. *In contrast to* the $14,560 Honda Accord, a comparably equipped Saturn only costs $11,620.

VOCABULARY CHECK

ECONOMIC TERMS	COMPANY TERMS	COMPANY ACTIONS
recession	profit margin	come out with
recovery	market share	launch
depression	borrowing costs	take off

READING
Answers will vary depending upon student's interpretation of Reading.

	GM	Ford	Chrysler
Product cost ranking	3	1	2
Management structure ranking	3	2	1
Finance situation ranking	2?	1?	3
Best in minivan segment	—	—	X
Tops in new marketing techniques	—	X	—
Strongest in Europe	X	—	—
Profits in nonauto operations	X	—	—
Weak in engines	—	X	—
Delays in introducing new models	—	X	—
Too many models	X		

SEGMENT 9

ON THE ROAD AGAIN

BEFORE YOU WATCH

PREDICTING

Sample questions:
1. What is the history of Harley-Davidson?
2. How did Harley-Davidson fall?
3. When did it fall?
4. Why did it fall?
5. How did Harley-Davidson rise again?
6. When did Harley-Davidson rise again?

KEY WORDS

Sample sentences:
1. When people think of the *establishment*, they generally think of companies like General Motors and IBM, not Harley-Davidson.
2. Companies often hope to establish brand *loyalty* among their customers.
3. For many people in the world, certain cars like Lamborghini, MG, and Corvette have a wonderful *mystique* about them.
4. Some people believe that the *classic* cars of 40 years ago look better than most cars on the road today.
5. *Implicit* in the statement that classic cars look better than those of today is the view that modern carmakers, for whatever reason, are not as creative as those of the past.
6. It is difficult for a company to make a successful *comeback* once it has done badly for a few years.
7. Sometimes a company will make a *desperate gamble* in order to make a comeback.
8. The *financial outlook* for Chrysler in the 1970's was extremely bad; Lee Iacocca did a masterful job of turning the company around.

GETTING THE MAIN IDEA

Who?	*Marketers of Japanese motorcycles*
What/do?	*They tripled production.*
What effect?	*Quality and sales went down.*
When?	*In the 80's*
How/manage?	*By creating new designs; by staying close to the customer and the product; by using techniques they learned from Honda*

WHAT'S MISSING?

1. question
2. fire
3. answer
4. fans
5. bike
6. popularity
7. Japanese
8. highway

WHAT DO YOU SEE?

1. empty road in the countryside
2. motorcycle gang
3. highway by the mountains
4. non-business people
5. man with a tattoo on his arm
6. old motorcycle on display

TRUE OR FALSE?

1. F Marlon Brando's *The Wild One* introduced *bad* boys on *bad* bikes.
2. T
3. T
4. F After 1954, Harley-Davidson was *the only* motorcycle made in America.
5. F Harley-Davidson motorcycles *have had* loyal customers in the past.
6. T

CHECKING WHAT YOU HEAR

1. √	6. √
2. √	7. √
3. √	8. —
4. —	9. √
5. —	10. √

MAKING TRUE SENTENCES

(The order in which the students make these sentences may vary.)

1. Japanese competitors offered more power, higher quality at lower cost in the 70's.
2. Harley-Davidson became a classic case of being left in the dark by overseas competition.
3. Honda came up with a very effective marketing campaign.
4. Harley-Davidson tried to cash in on the cycle boom by tripling production.
5. Honda implied in an ad that people who ride Harley's aren't necessarily the kind of people you'd like to meet.
6. Japanese competitors moved in for the kill when quality became a big issue.

PUTTING EVENTS IN ORDER

2. Harley executives borrowed $80 million to buy back the company.
5. The company got U.S. tariff protection against Japanese motorcycles.
6. Harley-Davidson came within days of going out of business.
4. The company created new designs, stayed close to customers, and introduced Japanese quality production techniques.
1. The company went through a lot of lay-offs.
3. Harley executives and investors went through some tough years.
8. The company began licensing the old name and appealing to upscale customers.
7. The company got a last-minutes reprieve from a finance company and a $20 million stock offering.

NOTETAKING

1. Bloomingdales
2. $10,000—middle and upper-income people
3. Professionals—insurance executive, teachers, banking CEO
4. Well-known, respected people
5. 1991–62%, 1985–28%
6. The U.S. market sales have gone down (it's shrinking)
7. Exporting to Japan
8. ". . . buy heritage, adventure, the lure of the open road"
9. Hollywood celebrities posing for free with their Harley's.

AFTER YOU WATCH

LANGUAGE POINT

1. Japanese quality production techniques are valued *not just* in Japan, *but* all over the world as well.
2. Harley-Davidson's story is *not just* an important one for American business, but for business organizations everywhere.
3. A company that stays close to the customer will *not just* change designs more quickly, *but* maintain its market share in tough times.
4. The Honda motorcycle in the 70's attracted *not just* many first-time riders, *but* also attracted attracted a clean-cut, upscale market that did not respond to Harley's tough image.

VOCABULARY CHECK

1. f	6. e
2. j	7. c
3. h	8. i
4. d	9. b
5. a	10. g

READING

1. Independence, freedom, adventure
2. By understanding its role in the American imagination and developing a unique relationship with its customers. They also shifted their focus to marketing.

3. a. Quality – Prove that the quality problems are over
   b. Niche – Define the niche
   c. Listen to customers
   d. Imaginative advertising
   e. Improve dealers (standards, training, penalties)

SEGMENT 10

FLEXIBILITY OF COMPANIES TO WORKERS' FAMILY CARE NEEDS

BEFORE YOU WATCH

PREDICTING

Sample items:

SIGHTS	WORDS
1. workers and their families	1. flexibility
2. examples of family care needs	2. benefits
3. examples of family care benefits	3. family care
4. women professionals	4. day care
5. company leaders talking	5. part-time vs full-time employment

KEY WORDS

1. g
2. e
3. d
4. c
5. a
6. b
7. h
8. f

GETTING THE MAIN IDEA

How?	They're offering benefits and policies that allow workers to balance job and family responsibilites.
Why?	More homemakers and people with family responsibilites are entering the American work force.
Why not?	They say the benefits are too expensive or not equitable, or that businesses should not be involved in family matters.

WHAT'S MISSING?

1. family
2. employees
3. problems
4. jobs
5. workers
6. women
7. companies
8. business

INFORMATION MATCH

1. e
2. c
3. a
4. b
5. d

LISTENING FOR DETAILS

1. c	6. b
2. c	7. b
3. b	8. c
4. a	9. a
5. a	10. b

NOTETAKING

1. No. Rebecca Chase says "most employees do not have these benefits because they are too expensive, cannot be used for everyone, or simply that business should not be involved in family matters."

2. These companies will simply lose out to those that do balance work and family.

AFTER YOU WATCH

LANGUAGE POINT

1. Because family matters are personal, some companies say that businesses should not be involved in family matters.

2. It makes sense for companies to offer family benefits because frustrated employees cannot focus on their work or careers.

3. Because some companies do not want to risk losing their top talent, they are willing to address these issues.

4. We have to fulfill their needs because recruiting and keeping good people is important to us.

5. Because HBO saves money by having the employee at work instead of having to hire a temporary, the company provides someone to look after an employee's sick child at home.

VOCABULARY CHECK (Matching)

1. c	6. d
2. i	7. g
3. h	8. e
4. f	9. b
5. j	10. a

CATEGORIZING WORDS

WORDS ASSOCIATED WITH CHANGES IN COMPANIES/CORPORATIONS	WORDS ASSOCIATED WITH MONEY
progressive	earnings
flexible	investment
innovative	expensive
revolution	return
restructure	account

READING

1. Main idea: "A tightening U.S. economy has forced U.S. companies to be more concerned with profit than with employee satisfaction and benefits."

2.

WORKPLACE ISSUES	Rating Received*
a. Cutting health care costs	**99%**
b. **Improving employee productivity**	97%
c. **Flexible working hours**	58%
d. Fetal protection from workplace hazards	**53%**
e. **Helping employees relocate**	50%
f. **Care for the elderly**	46%
g. Giving new fathers parternity leave	**45%**
h. **Providing jobs for spouses**	43%
i. **Offering job-sharing opportunities**	43%

*percent of managers who rated the issues important or very important.

SEGMENT 11

COMPUTERS AND CONSUMERS:
USER-FRIENDLY OR USER-SURLY

BEFORE YOU WATCH

PREDICTING
Sample kinds of information:
1. Changes that computers have brought to the workplace
2. Changes that computers have brought to the way people live
3. Kinds of problems that people have had with computers
4. Advantages of having computers
5. Disadvantages of having computers

KEY WORDS
Sample definitions:
1. *jargon*: specialized vocabulary that the general public does not understand
2. *disk crash*: the term for what happens when a computer destroys the data on a computer disk
3. *user-friendly*: easy for users to operate
4. *advocate*: one who feels strongly about something and tells others about it
5. *compatibility*: the condition of two different pieces of equipment will work well together
6. *training*: very specific education about practical matters
7. *back-up*: a spare copy
8. *psychic cost*: psychological or emotional frustration

WHILE YOU WATCH

GETTING THE MAIN IDEA

What?	Disk crashes, format failures, difficulty of use, destruction of data, compatibility problems, hardware failure, unplugged systems, etc.
How/feel?	They feel stupid.
What/cause?	The programs and the people that are selling them.
How/deal with?	They test the performance of hardware and software, they spend a lot of money on training and support; they keep printed back-up copies of everything.

WHAT'S MISSING?
1. failure
2. distance
3. computer
4. problems
5. 43
6. improving
7. U.S.
8. 35
9. friendly
10. users

NOTETAKING
1. That personal computers are still frustratingly difficult to use.
2. They think they must be stupid and that there must be something wrong with them because they can't figure out how to make the machine work.
3. The programs are stupid and the people selling the systems are stupid by not making them more obvious and easy to use and intuitive.
4. He can't get things to work.

INFORMATION MATCH
1. b
2. c
3. d
4. d
5. d
6. a

WHO'S WHO

Who. . . .?	Ronnie Davis	Chuck Eisler
1. is a small business owner	√	
2. is a theatrical producer		√
3. uses an Apple Macintosh computer		√
4. uses a Compaq computer	√	
5. had a 24-page proposal go to "Data Heaven"		√
6. experienced failure with a computer that held plans for a big dinner party	√	
7. now keeps a printed back-up copy of everything	√	
8. has thought of going back to using longhand, typewriters, and calculating machines		√

TRUE OR FALSE?

1. T
2. F The insurance benefits analysts were *unhappy* after their work was computerized.
3. T
4. F John Hancock was *not well* prepared for the calls and problems that happened.

AFTER YOU WATCH

LANGUAGE POINT
1. *Shut down*
2. figure out
3. get . . . out
4. picking up
5. going back to
6 crop up

VOCABULARY CHECK
1. c
2. a
3. b
4. b
5. a
6. b
7. c
8. d

READING
1. a. Unable to stop sending wrong bills
   b. Unable to correct an address
   c. Unable to divulge a piece of information
2. a. American Express
   b. "knowledge highway"
   c. To help people with every step of the job of managing credit, to shield both credit-card holders and employees from the bureaucracy needed to manage the vast business, so employees can be free to devote their efforts to building relationships with customers
   d. 1. Protects humans from error (every step of the way)
      2. Automatically pulls together all the information needed to analyze an account
      3. Reduces the number of queries the analysts have to make from 22 to 1

4. Keeps track of which state or national laws might affect the account
5. Helps to generate a dunning letter
6. Files all the paperwork
7. Automatically reminds the analyst if the account needs to be looked at again
   e. Instead of hiring people good at number-crunching and applying complex rules, it is turning to people who know how to deal with people
3. a. Compaq
   b. To improve customer service
   c. Installing automated assistants using "case-based reasoning" technology from Inference
   d. The principle that reasoning is often just a matter of remembering the best precedent
4. To build them them into the structure of the organization so that the work between people and machines can be redistributed
5. a. Can be expensive
   b. Must have tight integration between people and machines

SEGMENT 12
SHARING SWEET SUCCESS

BEFORE YOU WATCH

PREDICTING
Sample questions:
1. How does one company (or companies) achieve success?
2. How does one company (or companies) share their success?
3. What is the the philosophy of one company (or companies)?
4. What is the importance, or lack of importance, of a company having a basic philosophy?
5. What does one company (or companies) do to 'work smart'?

KEY WORDS

1. d	6. c
2. e	7. h
3. b	8. a
4. i	9. j
5. g	10. f

WHILE YOU WATCH

GETTING THE MAIN IDEA

Who?	Ben & Jerry's Ice Cream Company
What?	Integrating community concerns with making a profit
Where?	Waterbury, Vermont, U.S.A.
Why?	They believe they have a social mission
How?	They buy milk from a Vermont dairy cooperative; they buy brownies from a bakery which reinvests its profits into providing jobs and training for the homeless; they hire workers from every spectrum of the community; they provide on-site child care.

WHAT'S MISSING?

1. boss
2. stories
3. executives
4. laid off
5. economy
6. different
7. employees
8. Ice Cream

WHAT DO YOU SEE?

4 A sign that reads "Ben and Jerry's"
2 A picture of cows on the side of a building
7 A sign that reads "To make the world a better place"
3 A picture of the plane tearth on the side of a building
1 An icicle
6 A sign that reads "Leave no child behind"
5 A sign that reads "Take action here"

NOTETAKING

1. Vermont
2. The butterfat
3. Benefitting the community and making money
4. Super premium
5. 38%
6. Kraft Foods Frusen Gladje—3
   Pillsbury's Haagen Dazs—1
   Ben & Jerry's—2
7. Chocolate Chip Cookie Dough
8. a. $100,000,000
   b. double
9. 150%
10. $3,700,000
11. Quality control
12. One-on-one, through promotions or community events or things that tend to be more fun, for example, scoop trucks that drive around different cities in the country and just give out free samples all day, every day of the year.

TRUE OR FALSE?

1. F Because of the enormous growth in the past 10 years, Ben and Jerry have *turned over* most of the responsibility for the daily business operation.
2. F Anyone who takes a mangerial job at Ben and Jerry's knows that they *will not become* extremely rich if they do well.
3. T
4. T

5. T
6. F In 1990, Ben and Jerry's had to pay more than $30,000 in fines to the government for creating too much ice cream waste around the plant.
7. T
8. T

CHECKING WHAT YOU HEAR
  1. √
  2. —
  3. √
  4. √
  5. —
  6. √
  7. —
  8. √
  9. √
  10. —

AFTER YOU WATCH

LANGUAGE POINT
Sample sentences:
1. *Our mission* is to make profits and help the community at the same time.
2. *Our purpose* is to improve communication between management and employees.
3. *Our objective* is to reduce product defects, improve productivity, and increase sales.
4. *Our goal* is to become the top company in market share.
5. (any of the four ways) make the best products available at the lowest cost.

VOCABULARY CHECK
1. a	5. b
2. c	6. a
3. b	7. a
4. b	8. c

READING

1. Superior long-term performance
2. The beliefs, goals, and values that guide the behavior of a firm's employees
3. Strong cultures can help workers march to the same drummer; create high levels of loyalty and motivation; and provide the company with structure and controls, without the needs for an innovation-stifling bureaucracy.
4. That the popular view that a strong corporate culture always leads to success was "just plain wrong", because strong-cultured firms were almost as likely to perform poorly as their weak-cultured rivals.
5. Their managers do not let the short-term interests of the shareholders become the only goal, but instead "care equally about all of the company's 'stakeholders'," for example, employees
6. a. customers
   b. employees
   c. shareholders
7. It often takes many years to develop.
8. Appoint a boss who is unconventional or an outsider or both.